W9-CCT-448

ho ho ho

illustrated by mary engelbreit

written by patrick regan

**Andrews McMeel
Publishing**

Kansas City

MЄ MARY ENGELBREIT™

www.maryengelbreit.com

03 04 05 06 07 EPB 10 9 8 7 6 5 4 3 2 1

Design by Stephanie R. Farley and Delsie Chambon

ISBN: 0-7407-3905-0

Today's Christmas should
mean creating happy hours
for tomorrow and reliving
those of yesterday.

— Gladys Taber

Deck the halls
and hang the stockings!
Fill your heart
with Christmas cheer.

Make a wish and
mind your manners . . .
You-know-who will
soon be here.

He'll be landing
on the rooftop
with his bag
of toys in tow,

And come sliding
down the chimney
With a hearty
ho ho ho!

So be on your best behavior. Be both generous and nice.

Santa's got a list
   to track such things
(and they say he
   checks it twice!)

Put a shining star
   atop the tree
And presents 'round
   the base.

And to help
keep Santa tidy,
Clean out
your fireplace.

Bake some cookies!
Pour some milk.
Leave a snack,
    for goodness sake . . .

Santa's working awfully hard tonight—
He'll need a little break.

Grab your coat
and get your mittens
For a snowy
winter's day.

We've all got lots
we need to do,
But leave some time
to play!

Build a snowman
to greet Santa
With a carrot
for a nose.

It'll be a snack
    for Dasher . . .
Reindeer love
    to nibble those.

Then warm up with
hot chocolate
As you sing
a Christmas song.

Make the most of
every minute
'Cause this season
won't last long.

$\mathbf{N}$ow's the time for
making merry
There's no ifs or ands
or buts . . .

We'll recover from
it all next year...
Is Christmas
fun or what?